The Poetry of John Payne

Volume V – Thorgerda & The Fountain of Youth

John Payne was born on 23rd August 1842 in Bloomsbury, London.

He began his career in the legal profession but thus was soon put to one side as he began his renowned translations of Boccaccio's Decameron, The Arabian Nights, and then the poets Omar Khayyam, François Villon and Diwan Hafez. Of the latter, who he ranked in the same bracket as Dante and Shakespeare, he said; he takes the "whole sweep of human experience and irradiates all things with his sun-gold and his wisdom"

Later Payne became involved with limited edition publishing, and the Villon Society, which was dedicated to the poems of François Villon who was Frances' best known poet of the middle Ages and unfortunately also a thief and a murderer.

John Payne died on 11th February, 1916 at the age of 73 in South Kensington, London.

Index of Contents
THORGERDA
THE FOUNTAIN OF YOUTH
JOHN PAYNE – A CONCISE BIBLIOGRAPHY

THORGERDA

Voices in the Air

The night is riven from earth and heaven;
The day is blue in the sweet sky-dome;
The glad sea glimmers with soft sun-shimmers;
The white sea-fairies float on the foam.

The storm has faded from day new-braided
With webs of azure above the seas:
Shore-spirits, come, whilst the blast is dumb
And the seaflowers sway in the fragrant breeze.

I hear a ringing of sea-nymphs' singing,
Far out to sea in the golden haze:
Haste, sisters, haste, ere the noon have chased
The cool-haired dawn from the sweet sea-ways.

The air is golden; the storm is holden

In sapphire chains of the sleepless stars:
I see the flashing of mermaidens plashing
And merrows glinting in sea-shell cars.

Come swift, sweet sisters! Our witch-wife trysters
Will soon in the distance fade and flee:
Wide-winged we travel through the thin foam-ravel,
To ride on the weed-weft mane of the sea.

The Witch

Lo! what a golden day it is!
The glad sun rives the sapphire deeps
Down to the dim pearl-floored abyss
Where, cold in death, my lover sleeps;

Crowns with soft fire his sea-drenched hair,
Kisses with gold his lips death-pale,
Lets down from heaven a golden stair,
Whose steps methinks his soul doth scale.

This is my treasure. White and sweet.
He lies beneath my ardent eyne.
With heart that never more shall beat.
Nor lips press softly against mine.

How like a dream it seems to me.
The time when hand-in-hand we went
By hill and valley, I and he.
Lost in a trance of ravishment!

I and my lover here that lies
And sleeps the everlasting sleep.
We walked whilere in Paradise;
(Can it be true?) Our souls drank deep

Together of Love's wonder-wine:
We saw the golden days go by,
Unheeding, for we were divine;
Love had advanced us to the sky.

And of that time no traces bin.
Save the still shape that once did hold
My lover's soul, that shone therein,
As wine laughs in a vase of gold.

Cold, cold he lies and answers not

Unto my speech; his mouth is cold
Whose kiss to mine was sweet and hot
As sunshine to a marigold.

And yet his pallid lips I press;
I fold his neck in my embrace;
I rain down kisses none the less
Upon his unresponsive face:

I call on him with all the fair
Flower-names that blossom out of love;
I knit sea-jewels in his hair;
I weave fair coronals above

The cold sweet silver of his brow;
For this is all of him I have;
Nor any future more than now
Shall give me back what Love once gave.

For from Death's gate our lives divide;
His was the Galilean's faith:
With those that serve the Crucified,
He shared the chance of Life and Death.

And so mine eyes shall never light
Upon his star-soft eyes again;
Nor ever in the day or night,
By hill or valley, wood or plain.

Our hands shall meet afresh. His voice
Shall never with its silver tone
The sadness of my soul rejoice.
Nor his heart throb against mine own.

His sight shall never unto me
Return whilst heaven and earth remain:
Though Time blend with Eternity,
Our lives shall never meet again.

Never by grey or purple sea,
Never again in heavens of blue.
Never in this old earth—ah me.
Never, ah never! in the new.

For he, he treads the windless ways
Among the thick star-diamonds.
Where in the middle æether blaze
The golden City's pearl gate-fronds;

Sitteth, palm-crowned and silver-shod,
Where, in strange dwellings of the skies,
The Christians to their Woman-God
Cease nevermore from psalmodies.

And I, I wait, with haggard eyes
And face grown awful for desire,
The coming of that fierce day's rise
When from the cities of the fire

The wolf shall come with blazing crest.
And many a giant armed for war;
When from the sanguine-streaming West,
Hell-flaming, speedeth Naglfar.

I was a daughter of the race
Of those old gods the Christians hurled
From their high heaven-hilled dwelling-place,
Gladsheimr, poised above the world.

My mother was the fairest child
The Norse-land knew, so strangely fair.
The very gods looked down and smiled
At her clear eyes and lucent hair.

And Thor the Thunderer, enspelled
By hunger of a god's desire
For mortal love, came down, compelled
And did possess her like a fire.

And from the love of god and maid
There was a child of wonder born.
On whom the gods for guerdon laid
Gifts goodlier than lands and com.

There was to her the queendom given
O'er all the sprites of earth and sea,
O'er every wind that rends the heaven.
All lightnings through the clouds that flee.

Gifts did they give to her for flight
Athwart the crystal waves of air,
To cleave the billows green and white
And float among the sea-nymphs fair.

Her eyes pierced all the veils of mist
And all the crannies of the sea;

There was no hill-cave but she wist
To master all its mystery.

And since she was the last of all
The godlike race upon the earth
That could endure the Christian's thrall,
Being so mingled in her birth,

A spell was laid upon her life,
A charm of thunder and of fire.
That she should wage an endless strife,
For Thor the Thunderer's sake, her sire.

With that pale god, the Nazarene,
And all his servants on the earth.
Smite all their days with dole and teen
And waste their every work with dearth;

For that alone by sea and land
She should do battle for the gods
And for the Æsir) champion stand.
Far banished from the green Norse sods.

That child was I, Thorgerda hight
For memory of my mighty sire,
The last one of those maids of might
That ruled the fiends of air and fire.

I am the old gods' sword-bearer:
Upon this world of life and death,
Alone against the Christ I rear
The standard of the ancient faith:

I am their champion, that do wage
Unending and remorseless war
Against the new and barren age
That knows not Odin, no, nor Thor.

I am the witch of Norroway,
The sorceress that rides the blast,
That sends the whirlwind on its way
To rend the sail and snap the mast.

By day and night, by sea and land,
I wreak on men unnumbered ills;
I hurl the thunder from my hand,
I pour the torrent from the hills.

I stand upon the height of heaven
And smite the world with pestilence;
The Christ and his Archangels seven
Cannot prevail against me thence.

But more especially the night
Is given to me to work my will:
Therein, with ravening delight.
Of ruin red I take my fill.

When as the sun across the wave
Has drawn the colour from the sky
And over all the dead day's grave
The grisly night mounts wide and high,

My heart throbs loud, my wings expand,
I rush, I soar into the air
And falcon-like, o'er sea and land,
Valley and hill, I fly and fare,

I hover o'er the haunts of men.
Above the white town-dotted coasts,
The hollow, moon-bemaddened glen.
Brimmed with the bodiless grey ghosts.

I scatter curses far and near,
I fill the air with deaths that fly:
The pale folk tremble as they hear
My rushing wings that hurtle by.

And often, when the world is white
Beneath the moon and all things sleep,
I wake the storm-fiends in the night
And loose the whirlwind o'er the deep.

I sink the great ships on the sea,
I grip the seamen by the hair
And drag them strangling down with me
To drown among the corals rare.

I bid the volleying thunders roar,
The lightnings leap, the rushing rain
Swell up the sea against the shore,
To overwhelm the fated plain.

I stand upon the hills and hurl
The crashing thunderbolts afar,
Until the wild waves in their swirl

Blot out the sight of moon and star.

I slay the cattle in the stall,
I smite the sheep upon the fells;
The great pines in the forest fall.
Stricken and blasted by my spells.

The Christians call upon their God,
That cannot ward them from my power:
No living thing dares stir abroad
When as I rule the midnight hour.

No man that meets me in the night,
But he is numbered with the dead:
The world until the morning light
Is given to me for death and dread.

But, when the break of morning-grey
The cloudwrack in the east divides
And wan and woeful comes the day,
The tempest in my soul subsides;

And weary with the night's turmoil,
I seek some middle mountain cave,
Where sleep falls down on me like oil
Poured out upon the whirling wave.

Or else I cleave the glancing glass
Of the still sea and through the deep
Down to some sea-nymph's grotto pass.
Whereas the quiet corals sleep.

Unheeding if the sky is blue
Or if the storm in heaven is seen:
No whisper of the wind sinks through
The ceiling of that deep serene.

Sometimes, when heaven, frowning-browed,
Hangs o'er the earth, a leaden dome,
I cleave the canopy of cloud
And in the middle æther roam;

Seeking some token of my race.
Some sign to fill my void desire.
So haply I may see the face
Of Odin or my dreadful sire.

But vast and void the æther lies;

My wings arouse no echo there.
Nor my songs, ringing through the does,
Evoke an answer from the air.

Blank is the world: there seems no sign
Of all that was; the days forget
The gods that drank the wonder-wine
Of Freya's grapes whilere. And yet,

Behind the setting, now and then,
I see a crown of flame and smoke
Burn up above die fiery fen
Wherein, until the sable cloak

Of Time from sea and land be torn
And the Gods' Twilight fill the sky,
The Jötuns 'gainst the battle-mom
Forge weapons everlastingly.

And in my journeyings through the night
Across the billows rushing race.
Midmost the main, far out of sight
Of land, I come upon a place

Where in mid-ocean, storm-possest.
When with the sky the stem sea wars.
The Snake lifts up his horrid crest
And hisses to the pallid stars.

Bytimes, too, as cold-eyed I sail
Across the wastes of middle air,
A blithe breeze wafts aside the veil
Of clouds heaped up and floating there;

And dimly through the rift of blue
Turrets and hill-peaks I discern
And for a space behold anew
The golden gates of Asgard burn.

And as the vision grows, meseems
Valhalla rises grey and wide;
And dim and vast as thunder-dreams,
The old gods gather side by side.

Upon his throne of elfin gold
Allfather Odin sits: his beard
Streams o'er his bosom, fold on fold,
like mosses on an oak bolt-seared.

And an the gods around him stand,
Forset, Frey, Balder—ay, the dead
Joined to the live, an awful band:
And in the midst, with drooping head,

The semblance of my mighty sire.
Leant on his hammer, stands apart,
His sunk eyes gleaming like the fire
That glows within some mountain's heart.

A golden glimmer cleaves the gloom;
And momently, as if there rose
The sun upon some giant's tomb.
The haloed hair of Freya glows.

On Odin's breast she lies and sleeps.
Whilst, to his left and to his right,
A Valkyr armed the wild watch keeps.
By Friga, sitting stem and white.

Anon a Raven stirs and shakes
His sable wings athwart the hall;
And for a second Freya wakes.
And in their sleep the gods stir all:

And Thor lifts up his sunken head
And poises in his shadowy hand
His awful hammer; then, outspread,
Sleep falls again upon the band.

The Raven folds his wings anew;
The gleam of Freya's hair &des out;
And suddenly as first they drew,
The clinging cloud-wreaths fold about

The City of the seven-peaked Hill,
But I am glad for many a year:
For I have seen the gods live still
And looked on Thor the Thunderer.

And yet but seldom now the gods
Bow down unto my long desire:
But seldom in the sunset nods
Odin or Asa-Thor my sire

Strides on before me through the din
Of thunders in the midnight wild;

Nor on the hills the Nomas spin:
The gods are angry with their child.

Thor hides his visage from his maid,
For that, some little space whilere
Of days and nights, aside she laid
Her mission terrible and fair

And stooped to love as women love,
But fiercelier far than woman can.
The eagle pairing with the dove.
The heaven-born mating with a man.

It chanced, one summer's night of blue,
When only stars in heaven were
And like a lain of pearls, the dew
Slid through the golden August air,

My wings had borne me from the sea
To where the curving down sloped slow
Into a cirque of lilied lea.
Whereon sheep wandered to and fro.

Laid in the lap of cliff and hill.
The velvet down seemed fast asleep.
Save for the murmur of a rill
That trickled past the browsing sheep.

And now and then the herd-bells broke
The sleep of sound; and faint and far,
The ripple of the sea-surge woke
A languid echo. Not a star

Twinkled; but, in the drowsy dream
Of hill and down, it was as if
No storm was aye; and it did seem
No breakers roared behind the cliff.

The charm of peace that brooded there
Weighed on my wings; and wearywise
I floated on the quiet air,
Under the dreaming evening skies.

For momently the fierce delight
Of storm and vengeance died in me;
And some desire rose in my spright
Of rest and peace in days to be.

I was aweary of long strife:
The passion of my awful sire.
That had informed my lonely life
To wreak on men his dread desire.

Seemed weakening in me; and instead.
The earthly part in me arose,
Like to some fire that shows its head
Of flame above the boreal snows:

And as the keen heat melts the ice
And drives the winter-woe away.
So in my heart's fierce fortalice
Awhile the woman's wish held sway.

The godlike part in me awhile
Fainted; and in my woman's breast
The memory of my mother's smile
The empty place of hate possessed.

And many a longing, vague and sweet,
Welled up like fountains in the Spring;
My heart glowed with a human heat
And in my thought new hopes took wing.

Wish woke in me to put away
The wonted stress of doom and power,
That gave me empire o'er the day
And night in every changing hour

And made my soul a scathing fire.
An immortality of death;
And therewithal the soft desire
To breathe the kindly human breath,

To know the charm in life that lies,
To be no longer curst and lone,
To meet the glance of kindred eyes
And feel warm lips upon my own.

And as I wavered, half aswoon
With anguish of unformed desire.
The silver presence of the moon
Rose in the silence. High and higher

Into the quiet sky she soared;
And as she lit the tranquil sheep
And the pale plain, upon the sward

I saw the shepherd lie asleep.

Upon a little knoll he lay,
With face upturned toward the sky.
Bareheaded; and the breeze at play
Stirred in his hair caressingly.

The sudden sight to me did seem
The clear fulfilment of my thought.
As if at ending of a dream
The half-seen hope to shape were wrought

And day informed the wish of night:
For he was young and passing fair,
A very angel of delight
With sleep-sealed eyes and floating hair.

And as I gazed upon him, lol
The fierceness of the first love smote
The age-old ice in me with throe
On throe of passion: I forgot

My destiny in that sweet hour,
And all my birth had doomed me to,
Allfather Odin and his power.
The stars stood in that night of blue

And spoke of nought but hope fulfilled
And sweets of life with life new knit:
And through their glamour grave and stilled.
Love spoke and bade me worship it

I could but yield: the hot blood welled
Like balms of fire through heart and brain:
My every motion seemed compelled
To some strange ecstasy of pain.

So sharp and sweet the new wish was:
And as it grew, my tired wings closed
And down I sank upon the grass,
Hard by the place where he reposed.

Then, drunken with a fearful bliss,
I clasped my arms about his breast
And in the passion of a kiss.
My lips upon his lips I press'd.

The hot touch burnt me like a flame:

And he with a great start awoke
And (for sleep still his sense did claim
And the dream held him) would have broke

The prison of my clasping arms:
But could not, for aloud I cried
The softest, sweetest of my charms;
And as I chanted, white and wide.

My glad wings opened and I rose
Into the middle midnight air,
Like some night-hawk that homeward goes,
Bearing a culver to its lair.

The breeze sang past me, as I clave
The crystals of the sky serene;
And presently the plashing wave
Sounded, and past the marge of green

The long blue lapses of the main
Swept to the dawnward, and the foam
Slid up and fled and rose again.
Like white birds wheeling in the gloam.

Down through the deeps of yielding blue
I plunged with that fair youth I bore.
Harmless, until we sank unto
Where through the dusk the golden floor

And pearl-hung ceiling of a cave
Opened upon the sombre sea:
But by my charms the whirling wave
Drew back and left the entry free.

Therein upon a bank of sand.
Bordered with corals white and red,
I laid my lover. Cold his hand
Was and his face cold as the dead

And the lids fallen upon his eyes:
But soon my sorceries had drawn
The life back; and like some sweet skies
That break blue underneath the dawn,

His clear eyes opened on mine own;
he life-blood gathered in his cheek,
And gradually his fair face shone
And his lips moved as if to speak:

For at the first he saw me not;
But his eyes moved from side to side
Of that pearl-floored and golden grot.
As if with wonder stupefied.

Then, as they rested on my place,
At first, the pallor of affright
Drew all the rose-blush from his face
And made its brilliance marble-white.

But, soon, assured that I was fair,
(For of a truth new-born desire
Had bathed my beauty in a rare
Splendour as of ethereal fire)

A slow smile, gathering on his lips.
Broke into brightness, as the sun.
After some quickly-past eclipse,
Grows golden through the darkness dun.

His blue eyes glittered with soft light
And on his forehead's lambent snow,
The angel of a new delight
Brooded with pinions all aglow.

The passion in my veins that burned
Passed to his own like magic wine:
He raised himself with mouth that yearned
And eyes that fastened upon mine.

Then, as insensibly I drew
Nearer to him, moved by the spell,
About my neck his arms he threw
And on each other's breast we fell.

The dawn aroused me. To the dome
Of purine sea, that ceiled our cave,
The lances of the light struck home
Across the emerald-hearted wave.

Through weed and pearl the sheer sun smote
And turned the gloom of middle sea
To liquid amber, mote on mote.
Threading the air with jewelry.

And as the many-coloured rays
Played on his face, I leant my head

Upon my hand and fed my gaze
Upon my lover's goodlihead.

Long, long I gazed on him, entranced
With wonderment of dear delight,
Until the frolic motes, that glanced
Across his eyelids, waxed so bright

That needs his sleep must yield to it.
His fair face quivered, and his hand
Drew out of mine that folded it.
And then, as if some soft wind fanned

The petals of a flower apart,
That in their snowy bell confine
The dewy azure of its heart,
His blue eyes opened full on mine.

Once more the look of wonderment
Rose in their depths; but, ere it grew
Fulfilled, its faint beginning blent
Into a sun-sweet smile that knew

No thought save of perfected love
And happiness too sweet for speech;
And in that greeting our hands clove
And our lips grew each unto each.

Voices in the Air

We are glad for the golden birth of the noon;
We are filled with the fragrant breath of the breeze
The Day-god walks on the woof of the seas;
The green deeps laugh to his shining shoon;
And far in the fair sea-shadow the tune
Of harps and singings flutters and flees:
The sea-n3rmphs call us to follow soon,
To revel with them in the liquid leas.

All hail, sweet singers! We follow fast;
We follow to float on the white wave-run.
We stay but to finish the spells begun,
To rivet the chains of the bounden blast,
To seal the storm in the sea-caves vast
With the last few charms that are yet undone:
Then hey! for the plains where the whale sails past
And the white sea-nixes sport in the sun.

All hail! the sweet of the day is ours;
Our wings are wet with the salt of the sea.
Our task is over, our feet are free
To fare where the foam-bells shiver in showers
And the seaweeds glitter with glory of flowers.
The lines of the land do faint and flee:
We come to the heart of the mid-sea bowers,
On the race of the running billows' glee.

What power shall let us? Our lives are light;
Our hearts beat high with the laugh of the day.
We have sundered our souls from the dawning grey;
We have done with the dream of the darksome night;
We have set our face to the foam-line white,
To dream in the nooning the hours away.
Where the sea-swell heaves and the spray is bright
And the petrels wheel in the mid sea-way.

The Witch

My life put on from that sweet hour
Another nature: thence, no more
I thought to wield my baleful power
Nor treasures of my dreadful lore.

There was no magic now for me
In stirring up the stormy strife
Twixt heaven and earth and air and sea:
The memory lapsed from out my life

Of my dread mission: faded out
Was all my passion of wild hate.
My wrath ancestral, like a rout
Of dreams the sunbeams dissipate.

And I forgot the fearsome spell
That sealed my god-born life erewhen
With all the powers of hate and hell
To wreak the Æsir's curse on men.

The vengeance of the gods unseen,
Whilom with such a fiery smart
Kindled against the Nazarene,
No longer rankled in my heart.

The old gods died out of my thought.
As though in me they had no share:
The change Love had within me wrought
Blotted the past-time from my air.

No more I roamed the affrighted night,
Smiting the haunts of men with death:
The hamlets stood, unharmed and white,
Unblasted of my burning breath.

No curses slew the wandering folk
Belated on the wild sea-moors:
No pines beneath the thunderstroke
Crashed down among the trembling boors.

The sea slept calm beneath the sun:
No spells of mine across the sky
Unloosed the storm-clouds red and dun
Or hurled the thunders far and nigh.

But full and still the sunlight lay
Across the lapse of sea and land;
Save for the dancing ripples' play,
No surges thundered on the sand.

Love had transformed me: now I knew
None but his strife, no other bliss
Than in my lover's eyes of blue
To watch the coming of a kiss.

For him, I was an ocean-nymph,
One of the sweet fantastic kind,
That sport beneath the emerald lymph
And in their hair sea-corals wind.

Nought could his boyish wisdom read
Of my weird past within mine eyes:
For aye with happy love indeed
They bathed in dreams of Paradise.

And over all my haughty face
The glamour of the time had shed
A tender glow of timid grace.
The splendour of revengeful dread,

That once had marked me, was subdued
Into a glory faint and fair,
That rayed out from my softer mood.

Like sunshine in the April air.

All day within our cave we slept;
And when the sunset's scarlet shoon
Over the happy heaven swept
And in the faint-hued sky the moon

Mounted,—across the quiet land,
By hill and valley, wood and dale.
We wandered often, hand-in-hand,
Under the silver splendours pale.

And often, seated side by side.
Lost in each other's deep of eyes.
Insensibly the night would glide
Till morning glittered in the skies.

For nothing but our love we knew
In earth and air, in sky and sea;
No heaven to my gaze was blue
As that within his eyes for me.

I could not tire of his fair sight:
Whenever on his face I fed
My eyes, the first supreme delight
Relived in all its goodlihead.

And ever, when from sleep I woke
And saw him lying by my side,
The same sweet wonder on me broke
As when his beauty first I spied.

Ah me, how fair he was! Meseems,
Since God made heaven and earth and air,
He hath not in His wildest dreams
Made any creature half so fair.

About his forehead's lambent pearl,
Blushed with the rose-tints of a shell.
The gold locks clustered, curl on curl,
Like daffodils about the bell

Of some fair haughty lily-cup,
That in the marges of a wood
Lifts its broad snowy bosom up
And tempts the bees to light and brood.

And in its eyebrow's arching lines

Each deep-blue eye seemed, as it were,
A tarn dropped in a curve of pines.
Upon some snow-white mountain-stair.

No fruit was ever yet so sweet
As his sweet mouth, where day and night
For me failed never from his seat
The angel of fulfilled delight

No sunlight glittered like the smile
That blossomed from his flower-cup lips;
Whereat my thirsty soul the while
Did hover, as a bee that sips.

No snows of silver could compare
With the white splendour of his breast:
Whilst that my head lay pillowed there,
No angel knew a sweeter rest

His face to me was as a sun
That smote the winter-thoughts apart,
Scattering old memories every one.
And made new Springtime in my heart.

Love had brought back the age of gold:
For me, a new and fairer birth
Had made me radiant, as of old
Ask in the Paradisal earth.

It was as if a veil were drawn
That long had lain before my eyes:
Each hour upon my sense did dawn
Some splendour new in earth and skies.

The pageants of the sundown burst,
A new delight, upon my sense:
And night was radiant as the first
That fell on Embla's innocence.

The primrose-blooms of daybreak came,
A new enchantment, to my soul:
And noontide, with its flowers of flame.
Like philters on my passion stole.

Till that sweet time, the silver Spring
Had come and gone without my heed:
Nor with its flush of blossoming,
A glory fallen on hill and mead,

The royal Summer had prevailed
To stir the frost-time in my breast:
Nor yet the Autumn crimson-mailed:
Winter alone my heart possess'd.

But now each change of land and sea,
Each cloud that glittered in the sky,
Each flower that opened on the lea,
Each calling bird that flitted by,

Woke in my breast a new concent
Of deep delicious harmony:
My soul was grown a lute that blent
Its note with all sweet sounds that be.

My heart was grown a singing fire
That with each hour a new sweet strain
Mixed with the many-mingling choir
Of birds and flowers, of sea and plain.

My memory fails to count the lapse
Of time that held our happiness:
So full a mist of glory wraps
Its golden hours and such a stress

Of splendour folds it, that meseems
It might have been as time appears,
That in the dim delight of dreams
Holds in an hour a thousand years.

For all things 3deld to love fulfilled:
To those that walk in Paradise,
The falling feet of Time are stilled;
They know not if he creeps or flies.

A moment to their spreading bliss
May pass a century away;
Or in the passion of a kiss
A thousand years be as a day.

Ah me! though I remembered not
The seal my birth on me had set,
The wrath of Him that me begot
And the old gods did not forget

For evermore some omen sent
A thrill of anguish through my soul:

Some levin through &e dear sky rent;
Thor on the mountain-tops did roll.

And now and then, on our delight.
Across the amber wave would fall
The shadow of a raven's flight:
The great gods on their child did call

In wailing voices of the storm;
And in the sunset's gold and red,
Methought I saw the Thunderer's form
Grow in the gloaming, dim and dread.

But no sign rankled in my mind:
Love so possessed my heart and brain.
All else was but an idle wind,
A passing breath of summer rain.

One night, when not a zephyr's breath
Broke on the deep delicious swoon
Of hill and plain, and still as death,
The white world slept beneath the moon,

We tracked the quiet stream, that made
Its silver furrow through the strand.
And fell into the sea that played.
Lapping, upon the curving sand,

Up through wild wood and fern-grown fell
To where,—a silver thread across
The weeded pebbles,—like a bell.
Its fountain tinkled through the moss.

And parting back the lush sweet growth
Of waterweeds,—that there did cling,
As if the rivulet were loath
To yield the secret of its spring,—

We climbed through reed and fern and found
Where at the last the young stream shot
Its spire of silver from the ground.
Midmost a virgin forest-grot

The clustered clematis hung there,
Trailed curtain-like the place before.
As if some wood-nymph with her hair
Had made the grot a fury door:

And through the tangle wild and sweet
Of woodbind and convolvulus,
The silver streamlet, in a sheet
Of crystal multitudinous.

Poured arched above the entering,
And curving down across the roof,
Along the pearly floor did sing,
Threading athwart a tangled woof

Of moss and stonecrop, till it slid
Into a cranny of the stone.
Wherein it seemed the Naiad hid.
On green of leafage laid alone.

The place was sweet with jasmine-breath:
Across the silver-spangled grail,
Starred with blue blossoms, wreath on wreath,
Pervinck and saxifrage did trail:

And in the ultimate recess
A crowding growth of fragrant thyme
Had made a couch, such as might press
Some huntress-maid of olden rhyme.

The falling fountain of the stream
Alone the charmèd silence broke.
Like bell-chimes hearkened in a dream,
Unknowing if one slept or woke.

The drowsy sweetness of the place
Stole on our sense; and we, content.
Gave up ourselves unto that grace
And mingling charm of sound and scent.

Reclined upon that fragrant bed.
We lay embraced, perceiving not
Aught but the spell of slumber shed
From all that sleep-enchanted grot

And soon the tinkle of the spring
And the soft cloud of woodland scents.
That in the dreamy air did cling,
Laid hands of balm upon our sense

And sleep fell down upon our eyes,
As softly and unconsciously
As noontide from the August skies

Falls on the ripple of the sea.

He first did yield him to the charms
Of that sweet sleep and I awhile
Lay gazing on him till my arms
Relaxed and in my thought his smile

Blent with a dream of summer days;
And his face seemed to me a flower
That from the marging woodland ways
Bums in the golden noontide hour.

And so sleep fell upon me too;
The grot died out before my sight:
But yet the stream-song did pursue
My slumbrous senses, like some light

Chime of sweet bells in Faerie,
Threading upon a silver string
Of mingling dreams its rosary
Of pearls. But, as the crystal ring

Murmured unceasing in my ear,
Dulled with the dream, meseemed it grew
Slowly less sweet, less silver-dear:
A change across my spirit drew;

And gradually,—as with those
Upon whose head slow water drops.
Unceasing, till the soft fall grows
An anguish horrible, that stops

The pulse of life,—so in my brain
The ceaseless sound of that soft stream
Waxed to a terror and a pain
Within the chambers of the dream.

Methought at first it was a knell
That sounded for Love's funeral:
And then, again, its tinkle fell
Like storm-waves on a cavern wall:

But ever loudlier; until
It was the distant-seeming roar
Of thunder, over wood and hill
Growing and nearing evermore.

Louder and nearer still it came.

Until meseemed above my head
The bolts broke and the lightning's flame
Tore up the heaven with rifts of red.

And in the dream I heard the car
Of Thor across the hill-tops roll.
Shaking to ruin every star:
The world trembled from pole to pole

With that fierce clamour and the ah:
Rang with the startled nightbirds' cries.
And as I lay and listened there.
The Thunderer hurled across the skies

His awful hammer. Swift and straight,
Meseemed, it dove the screaming heaven,
Ruddy as flame, and fierce as fate.
Full at my lover's brow was driven.

Down at my very feet it fell,
Flaming, and cleft the quaking ground
Down to the immost heart of hell:
And from the rift, a roaring sound

Of fires innumerous burst into
The midnight air: the very core
Of the abysmal world shone blue
And awful. Then again a roar

Of thunders unendurable
The cloisters of the æther broke.
So terrible that the dream-spell
Was cloven in twain and I awoke.

The grot was still, save for the sound
Of waters whispering through the air;
The moonlight lay along the ground
And lit my lover sleeping there.

The terror of the dream possessed
My waking sense: with fearful ear
I listened, half affrighted lest
Some horror should be drawing near.

But not a breath the stillness clave:
The wind was silent: even the sea
Bore not thus far its rippling wave
And the birds slept on bush and tree.

Perfected peace held everything;
And yet there lingered in my head
The terror of remembering:
A cold sweat over me was shed

And my heart fainted in my breast:
I could not conquer with my will
The tremors that upon me press'd,
The thrill of thunders echoing still.

Some fearful presence seemed to brood
Above die place. Its every nook
Was lit with moonlight: yet I could
Awhile not lift my head to look.

At last, moved by some hidden spell,
I raised my eyes from off the floor;
And where the middle moonlight fell,
I saw a shadow in the door.

I could nor speak nor move for fear:
I could but gaze; and as I gazed.
The shadow darkened and drew near,
And from its depths two great eyes biased

Like fiery stars. Darker it grew
And taller, till the cave was filled
With the weird presence and I knew
The awful shape of him that killed

Skadnir; for now the dusk had ta'en
Terror and beauty; and before
My shrinking sight there stood again
The figure of the Thunderer Thor,

Leant on his hammer. Not a word
Came from the god's lips; bat his eyes
Blazed like a bale-fire. On the ground
I crouched before him, suppliant-wise,

With hands outstretched in silent dread:
For in the terror of his look
The anger of the gods I read,
As in some judgment-angel's book.

But still his eyes of changeless flame
Burnt on mine own; and as they shot

Their splendours on me, a strange shame
Rose in me, for that I forgot

The great gods banished from the earth,
The anguish of my mighty sire
And all the passion of my birth,
To follow forth a weak desire.

And as I looked upon him, still
The fulgent glory of his gaze
My every vein and thought did thrill
With memories of the olden days.

Before their searching light meseemed
The earthly part fled forth from me;
And it was but as if I dreamed
Love and its human ecstasy.

The woman's weakness of desire
Forsook my brain; and in its stead,
The old divine revengeful fire
Rose up within me, fierce and red.

Once more the wild wrath in me burned,
The passion of ancestral rage.
And once again my spirit yearned
To loose the storm-winds from their cage,

To cleave the quiet air with doom.
To ride the Sunder through the sky.
To chase the Christians to the tomb
Wi& lightnings darting far and nigh.

Then, as I rose, dreadful and fair
With that new fearfulness of birth,
The Thunder-god waxed brighter there,
Until it seemed the cowering earth

Trembled beneath his flaming sights
To me he beckoned, and I grew
In statue to my godlike height;
And still my steps to him he drew.

And as I strode out of the grot
And stood beneath the quiet moon.
Behold, I looked and saw him not:
But in the sky, rune upon rune,

The stars, in characters of blood
Shone like a scroll of fate and fear:
And as possessèd there I stood,
I heard the thunder drawing near.

Then, like some fierce volcanic sea,
The weird possession of my race
Rose, m3niad-minded, up in me.
One after one, like hawks that chase

Each other through the quivering air.
The spells, that startle from their rest
The tempest-demons in their lair,
Burst up, tumultuous, from my breast

And as they winged it south and north,
The thunder broke across the sky:
The snakes of doom shot hissing forth.
Crested with bale-fires blue and high.

And from the rifted clouds, that shone
Livid with sulphur-flames, there fell
Rain, hail and many a blazing stone,
As though to the sheer heaven hell

Had leapt, and surging o'er the world,
Like to a canopy of doom,
Upon the cowering valleys hurled
The fires and furies of its womb.

Then my wings spread out wide and white;
And through the turmoil I had made.
Drunk with wild wrath, into the night
I mounted. Many a meteor played,

Crown-like, about my haughty head:
And as across the sky I swept.
Like serpents following where I led,
About my path the lightnings leapt

From every comer of the sky
I heard the rush of flaming wings:
The fiends across the world did fly
And die air teemed with fearful things.

All demons in the earth that dwell
Or in the caverns of the sea
Gathered: the grisly ghouls of hell

And all the monstrous shapes that be

Within the air and in the fire
Flocked to my call, to wreak on men
The deadly passion of my sire
And the old gods: and now and then.

As, on the pinions of the wind,
Among the dragons I did stride,
With hair that flamed out far behind,
Methought I saw the Valkyrs ride.

And I the while chanted aloud
My sternest sorceries and hurled
My deadliest charms abroad and strowed
A rain of ruin on the world.

Each word I sang, each sign I made
Was fraught with terror and affright
Obedient, the levins rayed,
The hailstones hurtled through the night

A flood of fierce destruction rained
Upon the terror-stricken earth:
The hosts of hell were all unchained,
To whelm the world with death and dearth.

The ocean burst its age-old bounds
And rushed upon the shuddering shore:
As 'twere a herd of demon-hounds.
The whirling waves did leap and roar.

And soon no limit marked the place
Where the sea was and where the plain;
But over all the prospect's face
The raging waters spread amain.

And so all night I rode the blast;
And all night long, spell upon spell,
Rang, trumpet-sounded, fierce and fast,
My summons to the host of hell.

Until across the lurid gloom
A streak of wavering white was drawn
And like a grey ghost from the tomb.
Arose the pale phantasmal dawn.

Then from the world my sorcery ceased;

The demons vanished to the dead;
And at the token in the East,
The sullen ocean sought its bed.

Into the night the thunders died,
With wailing echoes o'er the hills;
And all the snakes of lightning vied
In flight before the morning's sills.

And then the pallid son arose,
Ghastly with horror: like a flame
On funerals its light that throws,
Across the wasted world it came.

Beneath its rays the earth spread cold
And stark as in the swoon of death:
The flocks lay dead upon the wold,
The cattle lifeless on the heath.

The homesteads lay in ruined heaps
Or stood a void of sea-stained stone;
Save where upon the mountain-steeps
Some bolt-seared castle rose alone.

And everywhere the folk lay dead.
Mother by daughter, sire by son:
No live thing seemed to lift its head
Under the epicedial sun.

Save where, perchance, a shivering group
Of peasants on some lofty crest.
Whither for safety they did troop,
Each against each in terror press'd.

No bird-songs hailed the hopeless morn:
The thrush sat dead upon the tree;
The lark lay drowned among the corn.
The cuckoo blasted on the lea.

The forests lay in tangled lines.
Smitten against the ravaged ground;
And out to sea, great rooted pines
Whirled in the eddies round and round.

Upon its seething breast, as 'twere
The trophies of that night of fear.
The hollow-sounding ocean bare
The drowned folk floating for and near.

Upon the waves their lank hair streamed
Like weeds; and in their open eyes,
As on the surge they rocked, meseemed
I saw the dreams of death arise.

Above the wrack of death and dread
I floated—like some bird of prey,
Worn with long rapine—in the dead
And stillness of the growing day.

And in my heart the fierce delight
Of ruin and destruction waned;
The drunken madness of the night
Ebbed; and but weariness remained.

Landward my tired wings carried me.
Following the rill, that now no more,
A silver ribbon, joined the sea.
But swollen into a torrent's roar.

Swept raging o'er its rocky bed:
And as I floated, knowing not
Whither, I saw that chance had led
My pinions to the river-grot

All bare it lay: the raging wave
Had stripped the creepers from the stone.
And in the opening of the cave
The rocky pillars overthrown.

The silver singing fountain-thread
Trickled no longer from the door.
An arching crystal: in its stead,
A foaming flood of water tore

The clinging clematiaes' woof.
The place lay open to the sky;
For in the storm the rocky roof
Was cloven and scattered far and nigh.

And as I looked upon the waste
Of what had been so fair a place.
With all its beauty now erased.
The memory of my lover's face

Smote on my spirit suddenly;
And in that flash of backward thought,

Remembrance startled up in me
Of all the change the night had wrought

The anguish of past love again
Revived in me; and mad with fear
And love foreboding, I was fain
To call upon him, loud and dear.

Across the air my shrill cries rang;
But no voice answered to mine own:
Only the calling echoes' clang
Rose up and died from rock and stone.

Again I called him by his name;
And still across the quivering air
The hollow-sounding echoes came,
For sole response to my despair.

Then, dazed with agonized affright,
I plunged into the surging wave,
That filled up to its utmost height
The hollow bosom of the cave;

And in the water-darkened grot.
With trembling hands and pallid face,
Madly I sought but long found not
My lover in that mournful place.

At last, as in the dusk I groped—
Probing each innermost recess.
To find I scarce knew what I hoped
Or feared—A floating tangled tress

Caught in my hands, as 'twere a weed
That in its flight the water bare:
But as I looked, I saw indeed
It was my lover's golden hair.

Then, diving through the pod of foam,
I saw, upon a mossy bed
That wavered in the watery gloam,
Where lay my darling drowned and dead.

Dead by my hand! In my embrace
I caught his cold form hard and close;
And spuming back the water's race.
Up to the outer air I rose.

And with all swiftness of my flight.
Across the desolated plain
I bore him, lying still and white,
Unto my cave beneath the main.

There, as the 'reavèd lioness
Moans, raging, o'er her stricken young,
Long days and nights my arms did press
The dead and on his neck I hung.

And all my sorceries I essayed.
If haply some imperious spell
The gentle spirit might persuade
Again in that fair form to dwell.

And many a fierce and forceful prayer
Unto the gods I cried and said,
That for my service and despair
They would but give me back my dead.

But every charm was all in vain
And to my prayers no answer came:
Only above the rippling main
Murmured in mockery, aye the same.

At last, worn weary of my life,
For uselessness of prayer and spell,
I did forsake the empty strife
'Gainst death and on the nymphs, that dwell

In every coral-wroughten cave
And every pearl and golden hall
That lies beneath the whirling wave,
With one last effort I did call.

Then came they and with hallowing hands
Bathed him in savours of the sea.
Bound his fair breast with silken bands
Made potent with strange balsamry.

And many a sweet and secret verse
And many a rude and antick rhyme—
Fraught with a spell—they did rehearse
About the dead, so—till the time

When like the flaming of a scroll
The heaven and earth shall pass away—
His perfect body fair and whole

Should know no vestige of decay.

Since then, the gods have seized again
Their full imperial sway on me:
For evermore, in heart and brain,
I am their maid by land and sea:

I am their servant day and night
To work on men their wrathful will.
To stand their champion in the fight
Against the Nazarene, until

That unimaginable day,
When in the throes of death and birth
The olden gods shall pass away;
When from the sea a new green earth

Shall rise, where in a glorious band,
Transfigured and regenerate.
The new-born heavenly ones shall stand
Before a new Valhalla's gate:

When I, content with ended strife,
Shall with my glorious kindred die.
Haply to live with a new life
In a new Asgard of the sky.

But lo! the night draws on apace;
The sun is sunken in the west;
And in the clouds meseems I trace
The scarlet-burning Serpent's crest,

Hurled up against the heaven. The flame
Of the gods' wrath bums up in me;
And through my veins a searching shame
Surges and will not let me free.

The maddening memory of my fall.
From the gods' service to the deep
Of woman's weakness, in the gall
Of bitterness my soul doth steep.

And as I overpass in thought
The time when I awhile resigned
Myself to love, my heart is wrought
To rage and wrath o'erwhelms my mind.

The bygone love for one man turns

To hate against the world of men;
Within my soul the old fire bums.
The thirst for ruin swells again.

Across the gathering gloom of sky
The dun clouds mass; and bade and forth
See where the calling ravens fly,
East unto west and south to north.

And lo! where in the sunset cloud.
Red as a sacrificial fire,
The form of Odin, thunder-browed,
Beckons unto my dread desire.

I know those signs: the old gods call
Upon their daughter to arise
From sloth and on the storm-wind's spall,
To ride the tempest through the skies.

The thunder wakens: Odin nods
And the sky blackens o'er the main:
My wings spread out: I come, great gods!
Your maid is wholly yours again.

Voices in the Air

The soft skies darken;
The night draws near;
I lie and hearken;
For in my ear
The land breeze rustles across the mere;
The corby croons on the haunted brere.

The sea has shrouded
The dying sun;
The air is clouded
With mist-wreaths dun:
The gold lights flicker out one by one:
The day is ended, the night begun.

The pale stars glisten;
The moon comes not:
I lie and listen
I know not what:
Meseems the breath of the air is hot,
As though some levin across it shot

The petrels flutter
Along the breeze;
A moaning mutter
Is on the seas:
A strange light over the billows flees;
The air is full of a vague unease.

Alas, sweet sister,
What fear draws nigh?
What witch-lights glister
Athwart the sky?
My heart with terror is like to die;
And some spell holds me: I cannot fly.

Was that the thunder?
A strange sound fled
And stinted under
The Westward red.
My weak wings fail me for dint of dread;
The silence weighs on my heavy head.

O help me, sweetest!
Of all our race
Thou that art fleetest
And most of grace!
The dread of the night draws on apace.
And we are far from our resting-place.

Lo, there a levin!
From shore to shore
Of midmost heaven
Hell-bright it tore;
And hark, the thunder! on heaven's floor
It breaks and volleys in roar on roar.

The witch! She rises
Higher and higher;
The gleam of her eyes is
A blue bale-fire;
Her stern face surges; her wings aspire;
Her gold hair flames like a funeral pyre.

Her incantations
Are in the air;
From out their stations
On heaven's stair
The angels flutter in wild despair;
The clouds catch fire at her floating hair.

Her spells have blotted
The stars from sight;
The sea is clotted
With foam-wreaths white:
The storm-clouds shut out the heaven's light:
Hell's peoples gather across the night.

The sea grows higher,
And evermore
The storm draws nigher,
The billows roar;
The levins lighten us o'er and o'er;
The fire-bolts hurtle on sea and shore.

Is there no fleeing?
Sweet sister, speak.
Hearing and seeing
Grow dim and weak.
Is't grown too late and too far: to seek
The land and the grot by the little creek?

I see death hover;
I cannot fly:
Is all hope over
And must we die?
My voice is failing: I can but sigh:
Can this be death that is drawing nigh?

I call her vainly;
She answers not:
Alas! too plainly
The cause I wot.
Her sweet face sleeps in the dim sea-grot;
The sea-snakes over her bosom knot

The weed is clinging
Her locks among;
The sea is singing
Her wild death-song:
Farewell, sweet sister! but not for long:
Upon me also the death-chills throng.

The stem sea surges
Against the sky;
Like sobbing dirges
The wild winds sigh;
My sea-drenched wings all powerless lie;

The light is fading from heart and eye.

The billows thunder;
The foam-bells flee:
My head sinks under
The raging sea:
The life is fainting, is failing me:
I come, sweet sister, I come to thee!

THE FOUNTAIN OF YOUTH

A ROMANCE OF THE SIXTEENTH CENTURY

We sailed from Cadiz, Perez, Bias and I,
Bound westward for the golden Indian seas,
One Christmas morning in the thirtieth year
Since Colon furrowed first the Western main.
Three old sea-dogs we were, well tried and tanned
In battle and hard weather; they had sailed
With the great Admiral in his first emprise
And I with stout de Leon, when he flung
The banner of the kingdoms to the breeze
Upon the sunny shores of Florida.
We had in our adventurings amassed
Some store of gold, enough for our require,
By stress of toilful days and careful nights
And dint of dogged labour and hard knocks;
And now the whitening harvest of our heads
Might well have monished us to slacken sail
And turn our thoughts toward the port of death.
Leaving the furtherance of our emprise
Unto the fresher hands of younger men.
But he, who long has used to ride the deep
And scent the briny breezes of the main.
Inhales a second nature with the breath
Of that unresting element and it.
With all its spells of reckless venturousness.
Grows subtly blended with his inmost soul
And will not let him rest upon the land.
And so we three, gray-bearded, ancient men,
Furrowed with years, but yet with hearts as stout
And sinews as well strung as many a youth
In whom the hot blood rages, launched again
Into the olden course and bent our sails
Once more toward the setting. Not that we
Were bitten by that fierce and senseless craze.

And hunger for red gold, that drove the folk
By myriads to the fruitful Western shores
And made the happy valleys ring with war,
Plains waste with fire and red with seas of blood:
A nobler, if a more unreal aim
Allured our hopes toward the Occident
And thawed the frost of age within our veins.

I had with Leon companied, when he
Sought vainly for the Isle of Bimini
And heard the Indians of the Cuban coast
Tell how, some fifty years agone, a tribe
Had sallied thence to seek that golden strand,
Where springs the Fountain of Eternal Youth,
And finding it, had lost the memory
Of all their native ties and lingered there,
Lapt in an endless dream of Paradise.
Oft had the wondrous legend stirred my sense
To intermittent longing, though, what time
The fire of youth was fresh within my veins,
I gave scant heed to it; but when my head
Grew white with winter's snows, the ancient fire
Flamed up again within me and my soul
Yearned unappeasably toward the West,
Where welled the wondrous chrism. At my heat
These two my comrades kindled to like warmth
And with like aim we fitted out a ship
And turned her head toward the setting sun,
Holding it well to let none know our thought.
But giving out we sought the general goal
And went to work the mines of Paria.
The Christmas bells rang cheerily, as we loosed
Our carvel from its moorings and the sky
Shone blue with blithest omen. So we stood
Adown the harbour and with favouring winds,
Came speedily to Ferro, where we took
New store of meat and drink and sailing on,
Had not long lost from sight the topmost peak
When some enchantment seemed to fall upon
And paral3rse the water and the air;
The glad winds dropped, the sea fell down to glass
And the gold sun flamed stirless in the sky.
For some score days we felt no breath of air
And heard no break of ripples, but we lay
And sweltered in the grip of that fierce heat
And so we drifted, in the weary calm,
A slow foot forward and a slow foot back.
Upon the long low folded slopes of sea.

Until, when all left hope and looked for death,
A swift sweet breeze sprang up and drove us on,
Across foam-spangled ripples, through a waste
Of wet weed-tangle; and anon the air
Grew faint with balmy flower-breaths; a white bird
Lit like a dream upon our sea-browned sail
And brought with it the promise of the land.
Softer and balmier grew the breeze and thick
And thicker came the signs of nearing shores;
And so, one morning, from the early mists
A green-coned island rose up in our way
And our glad hearts were conscious of the land.
Landing, we met with Spaniards armed and clothed.
Who brought us to the chief town of the isle.
That lay snow-white within a blaze of green.
It was New Spain, and having there refreshed
Our weary bodies with a grateful rest
Among the pleasant places of the isle.
We trimmed our sails anew toward the West
And steered into the distance with stout hearts.

Through many a winding maze of wooded aits
And channels where the lush boughs canopied
The lucent waters in their sanded bed,
We passed and smelt sweet savours of strange flowers,
That filled the forests with a blaze of bloom.
This coasting Cuba, and the last land passed.
Where the white headland rushed into the deep
And strove in vain to reach some kindred land.
Lost in the infinite distance, fields of green
Glittered and broke to surges, far and wide.
Until the eye lost vision. Nothing feared.
We bade farewell to all the terraced slopes
And fragrant woodlands and with fluttering sails.
Stretched out into the undiscovered seas.
Fair winds soon drove us out of sight of land
And in a sweet bright glory of June warmth,
Attempered by lithe breezes, did we cleave.
For many days, the slow and pearl6d surge.
Fair heaven o'er us of a wildflower's blue,
With now and then a trail of golden cloud.
Feathered with silver, sloping o'er its bell
Of windless azure, and a jasper sea,
Full of all glints and plays of jewelled light.
Fishes of diamond and seaweed trails,
Ruby and emerald, that bore wide blooms
Of white and purple. Some enchanted land
Lay for our sight beneath that crystal dome

Of hyaline inverted tow'rd the sky,
Drinking the soft light with so whole a bliss
That some new radiance ever woke in it.

So journeyed we for many a golden day
And many a night enchanted, till, at last,
One night, the sunset lay across the West,
In one great sheet of bright and awful gold,
And would not fade for twilight. Through the air
The hours fled past tow'rd midnight; but the sun
Was stayed by some new Joshua and the West
Still seemed the land of the Apocalypse,
Emblazoning the future of our hopes.
We all did marvel at the miracle
And some began to quake for very fear;
But Perez lifted up his voice and said,
"Friends, this is e'en the very sign of God,
To show us, of His mercy, we shall see
And come to what we long for, ere we die."
And. as he spoke, a fresher breeze fell down
Upon the gold-stained canvas of the sails,
So that we, driving fast toward the West
And its miraculous splendours, saw gold towers
And spires of burning emerald glance and grow
Against the golden background. Then great awe
And wondrous comfort fell upon us all
And from our lips, "The City of the Lord!"
Came with a reverent triumph, for it seemed
Indeed the town of pearl and golden gates
And angels walking in the beryl streets;
And as we ever ran toward the place.
The joy of Mary did possess our hearts
And kneeling down together on the deck,
We all linked hands and offered thanks to God.

The hours went by and lengthened out to days,
And yet no darkness curtained that fair fire.
No sign of dawning glimmered in the East;
But still that glory flamed across the West
And still into the setting fled our bark.
So, as we counted it by lapse of time.
Bereft of natural signs of dark and light.
Seven days had passed, and on the seventh day.
At fall of eventide, or what is wont
To be that time in this our world that knows
No miracles, the splendours gathered up
And running all together like a scroll,
Were bound into a single blazing globe.

That gradually did shrink upon itself.
Until it was but as a greater star
And hung in heaven, a splendid lucent pearl,
Flooding the purple twilight with soft fire.
And as the flaming curtain passed away
And left the Westward empty, from the span
Of ocean full before us, rose a slope
Of pleasant shores and smiling terraces.
Crowned with a tender glory of fair green.

Our hearts leapt up within us; something spoke
To us of the fulfilment of our hopes;
And as we drew yet nearer, snow-white sands.
Gemmed with bright shells and coloured wonderments
Of stones and seaweed, sparkled on the rim
Of the glad blue, and what seemed palaces
Of dream-like beauty shimmered afar off,
like agates, through the mazes of the woods.
We ran the carvel through a wooded reach
Of shelving water, clear and musical
With fret of breaking ripples on the stones.
And drove the keel into the yielding sand.
Where, with a gracious curve, the silver shore
Sloped down and held the ocean in its arms.
Landing, we entered, through a portico
Of columned palms, a forest fair and wide.
Wherein long glades ran stretching in the calm
And rayed out through the leafage on all hands;
And as our feet trod grass, the tropic night
Was wasted and the cool sweet early day
Was born in the blue heavens. On all sides,
The fruitful earth was mad with joy of Spring,
Not, as in our cold West, the painful lands
Flower with a thin spare stint of meagre blooms,
But with a blaze of heaven's own splendrousness
Moulded to blossom; in the lavish land
There was not room enough for the blithe blooms
To spread to fulness their luxuriance;
And so they ran and revelled up the trunks
And seizing all the interspace of air,
Shut out the sky with frolic flowerage.
And as we went, the cloisters of the woods
Rang with the golden choirings of the birds,
Gods' poets, that did give Him praise for Spring,
And all the tender twilight of the woods
Was brimmed with ripples of their minstrelsy.

Some hours we journeyed slowly through the aisles

Of emerald, hung with flower-trails wild and sweet,
Whose scent usurped the waftings of the breeze
And lapt our senses in a golden dream,—
Slowly, I say; for wonder held our feet
And we were often fain to halt and feed
Our dazed eyes on the exquisite fair peace
Of all things' perfect beauty and delight.
At last, we came to where the cloistered glades
Grew wider and we heard a noise of bells
And glad wide horn-notes floating through the trees
And waning lingeringly along the aisles;
And a far: voice of some most lovely sound
Held all the air with one enchanted note,
As 'twere the cadence of the angels' song.
When in the dawn the gates of heaven unfold.
Had floated down and lit upon the earth.
And then the forest ceased and in the noon,
Now that the sun rode high in the blue steeps.
We saw a fair white city in the plain,
Rounded with blossomed flowers and singing rills
And fringed with tender grace of nestling trees.
The gates stood open for our welcoming
And in we passed, but saw none in the ways
And wandered slowly onward through the streets.
Misdoubting us the whole might be a dream
And loath to speak, lest something break the charm,

Full lovely and most pleasant was the place,
Builded with palaces of purest white
And columns graven in all gracious shapes
Of lovely things, that harbour in the world
Or in the poet's fancy. All the walls
Were laced with golden tracery and set
With precious marbles, cunningly y-wrought
To delicate frail fretwork. Argent spires
Rose, pistil-like, toward the heavens serene,
From out moon-petalled flower-domes and the roofs
Seemed, in the noontide, one great graven prayer,
For the aspiring of their minarets.
Fair courtyards caught the quiet from the air
And hoarded up the shadow in their hearts.
Making the stillness musical with pearls
And silver of their fountains' gurgling plash.
A city of the pleasance of the Gods
It seemed, embowered in a flower-soft calm,
Soiled by no breath of clamour or desire.

So did we wander up that silver street,

As one who, in the lapses of a dream.
Goes like a God, for lack of wonderment,
And came to where a sudden water welled
Among moss-feathered pebbles and was turned
Into the middle way, wherein it ran
Along the agate stones, rejoicingly,
And marged itself with bands of vivid bloom.
It was so clear and sang so sweet a song
Of cool fresh quiet that we all were fain
To halt and lave our hands and feet in it.
So haply virtue might be had from it
Of its untroubled blitheness. This being done.
We wandered on again by that fair flood.
That seemed to us a rippled silver clue,
Unwinded by some river-deity,
Friendly to man, and leading, step by step,
To some far seat of exquisite idlesse.
So came we where the long slow quiet way
Was done and lost itself in one wide space,
Where columns stood in fair and measured ranks.
Arched with a running frieze of graven work.
Stately and tall they were, cornelian-plinthed,
With steins of jasper and chalcedony,
And ran in goodly order round the place,
Circling a wide bright curtilage of clear
And polished marble, veined with branching gold
And jacinth woven in its cloudless grain.
In the mid-square a cistern, lipped with pearl
And hollowed from the marble of the floor.
Was clear with crystal water, through whose lymph
One saw the bottom paved with cunning shapes
Of ancient legends, beasts and birds and flowers,
Fashioned in yellow gold on milk-white stone.

Into the cistern emptied all its rills
The laughing stream that ran beside our feet,
And filling all the cool still flood with gleams
And rippled swirls and eddies of its own
Mercurial silver, passed out o'er a slope
Of jasper from the cistern's farther side
And gurgled through a channel in the floor,
Wherefrom it drew that sweet and murmurous noise
Of soft accords suspended, that had swelled
Upon us in the opening of the wood.
Until its silver blended with the green
Of a cool woodland shadow and its chirp
Of laughing ripples in the cloistered calm
Of arching trunks was silent Following

The blithe stream's way, we stood upon the brink
Of that cool crystal and gazed down through it
Upon the inlaid figures in the bed,
That flashed and wavered so with that unrest
Of ceaseless currents, that they seemed to us
To have again a strange half-life in them
And nod and sign to us. We dipped our hands
For idlesse in the lappings of the stream,
That curled and glistered on the marble's brim.
And wondered idly what these things might be
That were so fairly pictured on the stone,
And if the place were void of living soul
To use its dainty brightness. So we might
Have stood and gazed and dreamed away the day.
So fair a spell of quiet held the air;
But, as we listened, suddenly a sound
Of various music smote upon our ears,
And we were ware of some enchanted throb
Of very lovely singing, that for aye
Drew nearer, as it were the singers came
Toward us, in the near vicinity.
And as it grew, the air was all a-flower
With intermingling antiphons of sound;
The passionate pulse of harp-strings, smitten soft
To wait upon the cadenced swell and wane
Of the alternate voices, throbbed and stirred
In the cool peace of that sweet reverend place:
High steeples rained bell-silver on the roofs
And the dear gold of clarions floated up
And echoed through the columned solitudes.

Before us rose a high and stately wall.
Painted with cunning past the skill of men,—
It seemed to us,—with shapes of olden time.
Presenting, in deep colours, like the flush
Of flowers that diapers the fields in June,
All things that have been celebrate of old,
Shapes of high kings, of heathen men and dames.
Ladies and knights in dalliance of love
Or ranged in rank of feast or tournament;
(I do remember once I saw the like,
But in a meaner fashion and less fair,
At Naples, when our army held the realm
Against the French). Surpassing fair they were,
Gods in the aspect and most worshipful,
Clad in bright raiment, gold and purpurine.
So goodly was their seeming and withal
So wonder-lively fashioned, that we looked

To see them leave their places on the wall
And walk among us and have speech of us.

Between two columns in the midst, a space
Was set apart, whereon no living thing
Was limn6d, but the stone was subtly wrought
With graven silver, arabesqued and chased
In interwoven patterns, very bright
And strange, wherein we wondered much to see
That ever sphere did twine with sphere, nor was
There any angled figure in the woof,
Except one great gold cross, that broke the play
Of circles in the centre of the space.
In this a wide door opened, that had been
So closely fitted to the joining wall
That our eyes had no cognizance of it.
And folding back itself on either side.
Gave passage to our sight into an aisle
Of cloistered fretwork, at whose farthest end
Shone glint of mystic gold and blazonry.

It was not clear for distance, at the first.
What was it moved and glittered in the haze;
But, as we gazed, a train of stately men,
Vestured in flowing garments, swept along
The heart of that cool stillness and did come
Majestically tow'rd us with slow steps.
And as they grew into our clearer sight,
We saw they were full goodly to behold.
Gracious in carriage and with port assured
In simple nobleness. It seemed to us
That we had known such figures in some dream
Of bygone days, so strangely bright they were
Of aspect and serene in kindly peace,
Resembling nothing earthly we had seen.
Their vesture was no less unknown to us,
Being of some fair white fabric, soft as silk
And looped with broad rich gold and broidery
Of banded silver, and their flowing hair
Was knitted with the plumes of strange bright birds,
That flashed and sparkled gem-like in the sun,
Emerald and gold and turquoise. At their head
Came one whose visage wore a special air
Of reverence and simplicity, uncrossed
By any furrow of ignoble care.
Adown his breast a fair white beard did flow
And foam-white was the flowerage of his head;
But else of sad wan eld was little trace

Upon his mien, except for venerance.
It seemed as if his youth had held so dear
The sojourn of life's spring-time, it had chosen
Rather to consort with the drifts of age
Than spread sad wings toward a fresher haven.
Upon his front a band of woven gold.
Graven with symbols, added evidence
Unneeded to his brow's regality.
And in his hand a silver wand he bore.
Whereon a golden falcon spread its wings
And poised itself as if for imminent flight.

We all bowed heads, as conscious of some might
Of soul and station far above our own;
And that mild ancient, casting on us all
His eyes' benignness, gave us welcoming.
In speech so clear and universal-toned.
We could not choose but apprehend his words
And the fair meaning of them, when he said,
"Be welcome to the City of the Day,
O seekers for the Isle of Bimini!"
And knew that here at last our quest was won.

Then did he speak to those that followed him.
And the fair youths, that were his chamberlains,
Laid gentle hands on us and led us all
Into the inner palace, where we soothed
Our weary limbs with soft and fragrant baths
And girt us in new garments of fair white.
Made rich with bands of silken broidery.
This done, our weariness and our fatigues
Fell from us with our travel-stained weeds
And we were as new men in heart and limb.

Then joyously we followed those our guides,
Through many an aisle of fair and lucent stone.
Into a wide and lofty banquet-hall,
Where the pierced walls showed through the azure sky
And shaped the light that won across the chinks
Into a dainty fretted lace of gold.
High up into the shadow curved the roof
And treasured up, in many a tender gloom
Of amethyst and purple, echoings
Of woodland songs and cool of forest shades
And soft sweet breezes straying in the flowers.
For bearing of its bell of latticed blue
Were columns of majestic linden-trees.
Whose blossom scented all the luminous air;

And in the boughs gold-feathered birds did make
Rare music for the pleasance of the folk
That lay below in many a goodly rank.
Reclined among sweet scents and lavish flowers.
There could no shaft of sun be wearisome
Nor airless ardour of the heavy noon.
For green of shading boughs and silver plash
Of ceaseless fountains in the hollow coigns.

Here was a goodly banquet furnished forth;
And as we entered, he that ruled the feast
Did set us near himself and talked with us
And showed and told us many goodly things
And marvels that had usance in the place.
Then did we ask him of that fabled stream
That had such puissance for defeat of age;
Whereat his visage grew, meseemed, a thought
Overshadowed; but anon he smiled on us
And made fair answer that, ourselves refreshed
With needful rest and slumber, he himself
Would on the morrow further our desire
Toward the fount miraculous; and turned
The talk to other things and bade us leave
Our past fatigues and eat and drink new life.

Great joyance had we in the pleasant things
That were presented to our every sense.
And great refreshing for our weary souls,
Jaded with age and unrelenting toil.
Nor, in the progress of the glad repast,
Did cheer sink down to grossness; for we ate
Of fruits and meats (and drank of wines the while,
Costly and rich) that were so delicate
And noble in their essence, and did hear
And see and scent such high and lovely things.
That all that was most godlike in ourselves
Did cast off imperfection for the nonce
And was made pure by that most sweet converse.

The banquet ended, minstrels took their harps
And sang the praises of the blossom-time
And high delights of bright and puissant love:
How May is sweet with amorous affects
And all things in its season know but one
And flower and sing and are most fair for one
And one alone most tender, holiest Love:
How life in love has ever deathless Spring,
And all the early glory of the year

Is but the travail of the earth with love,
That is told forth in bloom of painted flowers
And silver speech of many-choiring birds.

And these strains ended with applause of all
And to the great enhancement of our peace.
Another smote the soft complaining strings
To notes of graver sweetness and did sing
A quaint sad song of Autumn and of Death,
Made very sweet with joining cadences
Of silver harp-notes. Thus, methinks, it ran:—

Let others praise the May for bright and clear
And Love, that in the flower-time thrives amain:
For me, my songs shall hymn the dying year
And death, that is the salve of mortal pain.
For what is autumn but the grateful wane
Of weary summer to the sleep of snows?
And what is winter but the earth's repose,
And death the cold sweet close of some new Springy
That folds to slumber every tired thing?

Let others walk to hear the roundelay
Of song-birds quiring to the risen year:
 For me, I love the quiet throstles lay,
When in the woods the shredded leaves are sere
And the faint heavens are watchet in the mere.
The autumn's pale calm grey of sober peace
Is lovelier to me than the swift increase
Of colour in the spring-tide's restless air;
For my heart flowers when the boughs are bare.

If love be May, then lave is nought to me;
For in my thought his sweets are sweeter far
When in the deepening twilight shadows flee,
When all delights but half unfolded are
And waste fulfilment comes not to unbar
The gates of weariness. Faint flowers are sweet
And murmured music daintily doth greet
My senses more than bolder scent or song:
I will my Joys not fierce to be, but long.

Sweet death, if men do fear thy tender touch,
It is because they know thee not for fair,
Since that their eyes are dazzled over-much
By fierce delights of life and blinding glare
Of unenduring bliss, that throws despair
Behind it as its shadow, when the sun

Slopes through the evening and the hills are dun.
They would not call thee dark and wan and cold.
Had their faint eyes but shunned the noon's full gold.

For lo! thou art not black to loving eyes,
But tender grey, not unillumed by rose
Or that pale feathery gold that on the skies
Of autumn such a sad sweet glory throws.
Though in thy shades no glare of sunlight glows,
Yet through thy dusk a tender moon of hope
Is clear y nor lacks there in the misted slope
Of thy long vistas many a helpful light,
O Death, for very piteous is thy might!

Let those that love them sing of Love and May;
I give to Love full sweet another name
And with soft sighs and singings to Him pray,
And not with trumpets silver-strong acclaim
Blazon to men his wonder-working fame:
For my Love's name is Death, and I am fain
To love the long sad years and life's kind wane;
For what is autumn but a later Spring
And what is Death but lifers revesturing?

Thus blithely sped the golden-footed hours
Athwart the sloping sunlight of the space
Twixt noon and dusk, in various delight
Of song and converse, till the purple webs
Of night began to flutter o'er the gold
Of sunset, and the air of that bright place
Was strewn with pearls of moonlight. Then men brought
Great golden-fleec6d webs of silk-soft wool
And furs of white and sable-coated beasts
And laid them on the floor and thereon strewed
Fair green of moss and rainbow plumages
Of exquisite strange birds, whereon the folk.
Won with light labour to fatigue as light
And easeful, soon addressed themselves to rest.

But those fair youths, to whom we were in charge,
Unbidden, brought us to a place apart,
Wherein fair chambers, golden-ceiled and hung
With gray and purple arras, lay beside
An aisle of columned marble, stretching down,
With casements clear and quaintly-carven roofs.
Through many a tender vista of soft shade
And trellised leafage: there did we bestow
Our weary limbs and heard the nightingale,

All night among the windless myrtle-groves
Without, entreating all the tremulous air
To passion with the splendour of her song.
Woven with flower-scents inextricably.
The night was fair for us with happy dreams.
And in the morning, ere the sun had drawn
The early mists from off the blushing day,
There came to us the king of that fair land
And did entreat us rise and harness us;
For that the place we sought was from the town
Distant a long day's journey, and the time
Was gracious, in the freshness of the dawn,
To break the earlier hardness of the way.
Then did we all take horse and riding forth
By the fair guiding silver of the brook.
That ran toward the northward of the town.
We passed through many a leafy forest glade
And saw the fresh flowers wet with the night dew
And listened to the newly-wakened birds.
That sang their clearest for the fair young day.
Right goodly was the aspect of the earth.
Clad with glad blooms and flushed with joy of Spring,
As on we wended in the early morn.
Before the grossness of the noon fell down:
And as we went, a goodly company.
The minstrels lifted up their voice and sang.
As birds that could not choose but music make.
For very joyance of the pleasant time.
And one right well I marked, who made the birds
From every sunny knoll and budded copse
Give back blithe antiphons of melody
To every phrase and cadence of his song.
Comely and young he was and passing skilled
In making lays and rondels for the lute:—
And this, among a crowd of sweeter songs,
If memory serve me rightly, did he sing.

Bells of gold where the sun has been,
Azure cups in the woven green,
Who in the night has been with you
And painted you golden and jewel-blue
And brimmed your flower-cups with diamond dew?

Lo! in the evening Spring was dead
And the flowers had lost their maidenhead
Under the burning kiss of the sun:
Tell me, who was the shining one
That came by nighty when the sky was dun

And the pale thin mists were over the moon,
And brimmed your hearts with the wine of noon?
Who was it breathed on the painted May,
Under the screen of the shadow play,
And gave it life for another day?

I watched at the setting to see him ride.
But only saw the day that died,
The faint-eyed flowerets shrink and fail
Into their shrouding petals' veil
And all things under the moon turn pale.

I watched in the nighty but saw no thing,
I heard in the midnight the grey bird sing
And ran to look for the shape of power,
But saw no thing in the silence flower,
Save moonmists over forest and bower.

Goldcups, it could not have been the May,
For dead in the twilight the Spring-time lay,
Under the arch of the setting sun,
Ere in the gloaming the day was done
And the masque of the shadows had begun.

Bui lo! in the early scented morn
A new delight in the air was born;
Brighter than ever bloomed the Springy
The glad flowers blew and the birds did sing
And blithe was every living thing.

Merles that flute in the linden-hall,
Larks, if ye would, ye could tell me all;
Ye that were waking at break of day.
Did ye see no one pass away.
With ripple of song and pinion-play?

Ah! I am sure that ye know him welly
Although ye are false and will not tell!
Haply, natheless, I shall be near
And hear you praise him loudly and clear,
Some day when ye wit not I can hear.

So wended we with mirth and minstrelsy
Throughout the morning hours, and presently
Emerging from the pleasant wood, we rode
By many a long stretch of level plains,
Waved fields of rainbow grasses and wide moors

Bejewelled thick with white and azure bells,
And saw rich flowercups, all ablaze with gold
And purple, lie and swelter in the sun,
And others, blue as is the sky at noon
Unclouded, trail and crawl along the grass
And star the green with sudden sapphire blooms.
And then we came to where the frolic brook
Swelled into manhood and its silver thread
Was woven out into a river's stretch
Of broad, unruffled crystal. Here a boat,
Wide bowe4 and long, lay rocking on the stream,
Among great lazy lilies, white and red
And regal purple, lolling in the sun.

Dismounting here, we floated up the tide.
Propelled by one that stood upon the prow
And spumed the sanded bottom with his pole,
Along wide sunny lapses of the stream,
Now breasting rushes, purple as the tips
Of fair Aurora's fingers, when she parts
The veils of daybreak, now embowered in green
And blue of floating iris. Through long rifts
Of wooded cliffs we passed, where here and there
The naked rock showed white as a swan's breast,
Riven through and through by veins of virgin gold,
Or haply cleft with gaping crevices.
Wherethrough the jewelled riches of its heart
Did force themselves from out their treasury
And staunched the cloven wound with precious salve
Of living diamond. Here the water showed,
Through its clear lymph, great crystals in the bed
And nuggets of bright metal, water-worn
To strange fantastic shapes; and now and then,
As we did paddle idly with our hands,
Letting the clear stream ripple through the chinks
Of our obstructing fingers, with a sound
Of soft melodious plaining for the check,
A great gold-armoured fish, with scales of pearl
And martlets of wine-red upon his back,
Rose slowly to the surface, waving all
The pennons of his fins, and gazed at us
With fearless eyes. And there the wrinkled bed
Shelved suddenly into a deep clear pool,
Whose brink was fringed with waving water-bells;
And at the bottom lay gold-coloured shells
And silver pearls embedded in brown sand,
And many a fish and harmless water-snake

Floated and crawled along the river-weeds.

But nothing harmful seemed to us to dwell
Within that fair clear water;—pike nor coil
Of deadly worm, nor on the verging banks
In field or copse, as far as eye could see,
Was any lynx or wolf or brindled beast,
To stir the lovely stillness of the land
With whisper of disquiet. As we went.
Much wondering at the goodly peace that reigned
In all and at the marvellous fair things
That glided by us, Perez took a lute
(Full featly could he turn a stately song,)
And praised the place and its serene delights.

"O happy pleasaunce of the gods!" he sang,
"'Where all is fair and there is harm in nought,
Where never lightnings break nor thunder-clangy
Nor ever summer air with storm is fraught,
Nor by the hurtling hail is ruin wrought,
But kindly nature is at peace with man
And all things sweetly fill their given span!

"O pleasant land, where winter never blinds
The bare waste ways with snowdrift, nor the frost
With wrinkled ice the sad wan waters blinds
Nor Spring-tide joy by winter thoughts is crost,
Where never hope for weariness is lost,
But life is warm, though woods be cold and grey,
And never in the flower-hearts dies the May!

"Where never skies are dull, nor tempest scowls,
Nor monster riots in the river's glass.
Where never in the woods the fierce beast prowls,
But in the fields the harmless snake does pass,
A living jewely through the flowered grass,
Where sun burns not, nor breaths of winter freeze,
Nor thunder-blasts shrill drearly through the trees!

"Yet is there nothing here that in the air
Should breathe such potency of healing balm
As might compel the unkindly blast to spare
Or birds to sing a never-ending psalm,
Or meadows glitter with the summer calm,
Or purge the terror from the winter grim:
But men love God and put their trust in Him!

"And so all things of His do they hold dear

And see in all His handiwork a friend,
And not a foe—and therefore skies are clear
And flowers are sweet, because men's souls intend
The essence of well-being and so bend
The kindred life of wood and field and fell
To that fair peace that in themselves does dwell!

"For man it is that makes his circumstance,
Honouring all and loving all things good,
Bethinking him how he may best advance
The harvesting of natures kindly mood,
By helping her in that relief she would
Be ever working for his cheer and stay:
So doth he love and joy in her alway.

"O happy folk that dwell in such a land!
O happy land that hast such habitants,
That know to walk with nature hand in hand
And find new cheer in every change and chance,
Not thinkings when the long grey days advance
And summer's gold is dyings hope is less;
But proving lightly all things' goodliness,"

So swung we slowly up that lazy flood,
Rejoicing in the gladness of the time,
Until its course did leave the open plains
And turned into a forest, intertwined
So closely o'er our heads with knitted boughs
And charm of woven leaves, that we could see
No glimpse of sun nor glitter of the clear
Sweet firmament, nor any moving thing,
But only heard dim splashes in the flood
Of water-rat or duck and distant chirp
Of birds that far above our heads climbed up
To hymn the mounting chariot of the sun.

In that dim emerald shadow, some strange peace
And spell of haunting quiet seemed to brood
And soften all the voices of the wood
And rustle of the leafage to repose.
Above us rose the high steep flowered banks,
Heavy with fragrances from unseen bells
Exhaled of sweet and drowsy-scented flowers.
And all around the columns of the trees
Stretched dimly in the twilight, like the aisles
Of some immense cathedral, where the voice
Of praise and joy is hushed to reverent prayer.
And there no bird or beast did seem to dwell

Nor breeze to creep and sigh among the trees;
But in its own mysterious sanctity
The forest lay and waited for the voice
Of some high champion that should break the charm
And win the secret of those mystic deeps.

The air grew darker, and a fresher breeze
Sprang up and told us of the waning day;
And then the oarsman laid aside his blade
And loosed the wide sail from the tapering mast.
Wherein the glad air gathered did so swell
And struggle, that the boat leapt swiftly on
Between the shelving woodways. And anon
The gold of sunset flamed in through the mask
Of thinning trees, and then the prow was free
From that dark pass of overhanging wood,
And the day's light was large on us again.

The river lapsed, thro' fringing marish plants
And ranks of rustling reeds, into the glass
Of a clear lakelet, where the white discs lay,
Gold-hearted, in the quiet, and our stem
Cut through the fronded lake-weeds grudgingly
And won slow way toward the other shore.
Where, with a hollow roar, the river leapt
And fell into a dark and shaded cave.

There landed we and moored the barge with ropes,
And following our guides, made shift to win,
Athwart a rocky passage, to a screen
Of netted boughs and bushes that shut out
For us the blue horizon's golden marge.
Some time we struggled through the arduous growth
Of underwood and brambles, intertwined
With scarlet-blossomed creepers, till at length
The last boughs closed behind us and we stood
Upon the lower slope of a tall hill
And gazed into the sunset with rapt eyes.

A wide deep champaign stretched before our view,
Encircled with a sapphire chain of hills.
On whose high crests the crown of sunset lay,
Hallowing the landscape with a blaze of gold.

Fair and most awful was the majesty
Of that day's death upon the guardian hills.
Wrapt in the visible glory of the Lord;
And with one impulse, as the budded flames

Of imminent heaven lay on us, we all
Fell down upon our knees and worshipped.
As knowing the great God was surely there.

So knelt we all in silence, till the sun
Had faded from the westward and the grey.
Washed with pale gold, that fills the interspace
Twixt ended day and night, held all the air
With its mild tender afterglow. Then he
Whose brow was kingly with the banded gold
Arose and went a little way aside
Within some trees, that stood apart from us
About the casting of an arbalest,
And made as if he sought for something there;
And coming, in a little, back to us,
He took my hand, and signing to the rest
To follow, led us all into a nook.
Wherein tall oak-trees circled round a rock
Of moss-veined marble. Therein entering,
A fitful radiance, as it were the play
Of glancing diamonds, glittered in our eyes.
And looking round, we saw where from the stone
A fair clear water trickled, drop by drop.
Between lush webs of golden-threaded moss,
And fell in jewelled sprays of liquid light
Upon the crystal pebbles. Very pure
And clear it was and so unearthly bright
In the dim twilight of that shadowy place.
We doubted not but here our quest was filled
And this was e'en that fountain where our flesh.
Being laved, should put off sad and weary age
And clothe itself anew with goodly youth.
Then he who led us signed to us to drink.
For this was that same water we had sought
And wearied for so long by sea and land.

Albeit, for a space we could not stir
For wonderment, commingled with strange awe
And ravishment of our fulfilled desires.
That was nigh pain for very mightiness.

And then Bias stepped toward that trickling thread
Of crystal and did stoop him down to drink;
And ere his knees touched earth, I, following.
Bent down my hand into the rippled pool,
That lay beneath the downfall of the rill.
And drawing back an instant for surprise
At the most deathly coldness of the stream,

Made shift to gather water for a draught
Within the hollowed middle of my palm.

It scattered into diamonds through the chinks
Of my unnervèd fingers and did leave
So scant a pool of fluid in my hand,
That I was fain to stoop and fill again,
With more attent precaution, ere I wet
My lips with it. I filled my two joined palms
And was about to raise them to my mouth,
Nay, almost steeped my lips, when suddenly.
Reflected in the streamlet, I was ware
Of some strange light that was made visible
From out the dusk above, and looking up,
I spied a moonèd wonder in the air.
Full of strange lights and mystic harmonies
Of blending colour; and as I did gaze,
I saw a great white cross, that grew and burnt
In its fair middle. Wonder and great awe
Unclasped my hands and brought them to my face,
To hide from my weak sight that awful light.
Whereby the unwilling water once again
Did have its liberty and showered down.
Like broken jewels, back into the pool
And as I knelt, with awed and hidden eyes,
I heard a voice that spake from out the bell
Of that miraculous flower, most reverend
And awful, as it were the living God;
And these words smote my hearing: "Foolish men,
That thought God like another of yourselves,
That make a work and set it up for good
And after look again and know it ill
And straightway raze and build it up anew,
Repenting of the framework of your hands,—
Know that the Lord of all cannot repent
Nor turn again His ordered harmonies
Of life and death and Nature, saying not,
'I have not wrought it seemly—I repent
Nor can His hands undo what He has done,

"O fools and hard of heart I in all these years
Have ye then never read earth's parable
Of day and night alternate, seed and fruit,
That tells you dusk must be ere light can comet
Lo, in the fields the summer's lavish bloom
Is spent and wasted by the autumn's breath
And dies with winter, to revive with spring;
And all things fill their order, birds and beasts

And all that unto earthly weal pertains.
Nor will the spheric working change its course
Nor slacken for the prayers of foolish men,
That lift fond voice for what their baby eyes
Deem good and all-sufficient in desire,
Seeing only, in their circumscribèd scope,
A segment of the circle of God's love.

"So may not the renewing of lost youth
Be won but through the natural way of deaths
And man must,—like an ear of corny that droops
And withers in the ground before it stir
And sprout again with gay and goodly bloom,—
Yield up his wayworn flesh and weary soul
Unto the soothing rest of friendly deathy
Ere a new fire shall stir the curdled blood
Of age to a new ardour and the soul
Be clad afresh with robes of lusty youth.

"Wherefore know ye that, of a certainty,
None shall have life, excepting first he die.
And therefore is this water cold as death;
For through its death is life the quicklier won.
Wherefore, if ye repent of your desire
And will to wear in weariness of eld
The sad remainder of your lagging years,
Rather than dare the icy plunge of death,
Depart and purge your hearts of foolish hope."

With that it ceased: and we, for wonderment
And awe, awhile could neither move nor speak;
But still that splendour hung upon the air
And still we veiled our eyes for reverence.

Then Perez rose and coming to the brink
Of that miraculous water, knelt and said;
"Lord, I have haste for youth and fear not death,
For joy of that great hope that is beyond."

So lightly he addressed himself to drink
Of that clear stream; and we, that watched him do,
When as the water touched him, saw his face,
As 'twere an angel's, with heroic love
And faith transfigured for a moment's space;
And then such glory broke from that high cross
And shone athwart his visage, that we fell
Aswoon upon the grass for fear and awe
And had no further sense of what befell.

When life again returned into my brain,
The night was wasted, and the early dawn
Was golden in the Orient. As my eyes
Grew once more open to the light of day,
I found myself outstretched upon the sand
Of that fair shore, where we had landed first,
Hard by our place of entry in the wood.

Around me were my comrades; some, like me,
Awaking from the trance of that strange sleep
And others working on the caravel,
That lay high up upon the waveless strand.
Striving to push her down to meet the tide
That crawled up slowly from the outer sea.

But every sign of our adventurings
In that fair city, with those goodly men,
And of that wondrous fountain of the hills,
Was vanished. In the tangles of the wood,
The fair white dwellings we had seen with eyes,
When first the sunset led us to the place,
Had disappeared, nor in the forest's close
Green front of woven boughs, that stood opposed
Toward the ocean, was there visible
A single opening, wherethrough we might chance
Again upon the cloistered woodland way,
That led us to the wonder-lovely town.
Nor was there any sign or any trace
Of habitance of men or mortal use
Therein: but all was as no human foot.
Save ours, had trodden on the silver sand.

At this we marvelled greatly and most like
Would have misdoubted all to be a dream,
But that there lay beside us on the strand
Our comrade, Perez, not,—as first it seemed
To us,—asleep, but,—as we soon knew,—dead.
And still his visage wore the wondrous smile
Of deathless ravishment it had put on
With the clear draught of that miraculous fount.

And so we knew that it had been no dream.
But that our eyes had seen our hearts' desire
And God Himself had surely talked with us.

Long with persistent hope we searched the shore
Around the little harbour on all sides.

So haply we might once more light upon
The woodway leading to the inland plain
And its blithe wonders: but the silent trees
Were secret and would show no trace of it.

And so with heavy hearts we left our search
And made a grave for burial of the dead
And laid him there with a sad reverence.
With wail and music of a funeral song;
For very dear the man had been to us.
Being of a noble nature and approved
In all renown of worth and steadfastness.

Then sadly from a little smooth-stemmed tree
We rove a branch and hewing it in twain.
Made shift to fashion of the peeled white wood
The rude resemblance of the blessed Rood
And planted it for memory on the grave.
And as we did this thing, the forest air
Was voiceful with the carol of a bird.
That piped and piped as though he ne'er should die.
So joyous was his song and full of hope,
It seemed as if the angel of the dead
Had entered in the semblance of a fowl
And sang to give us lightening of our grief

And so it came to pass that with the song
Our hearts were comforted and some did deem
They saw himself that stood upon the strand
And beckoned to us not to tarry there
Nor strive against the given will of God,
But turn our prow from off that hallowed shore.

We waited not for bidding, but launched out
And made the swift keel whistle through the surge.

John Payne – A Concise Bibliography

The Masque of Shadows & Other Poems (1870)
Intaglios; Sonnets (1871)
Songs of Life and Death (1872)
Lautrec: A Poem (1878)
The Poems of François Villon (1878)
New Poems (1880)
The Book of the Thousand Nights and One Night (1882–4) A translation in nine volumes
Tales from the Arabic (1884)

The Novels of Matteo Bandello, Bishop of Agen (1890) A translation in six volumes
The Decameron by Giovanni Boccaccio (1886) A translation in three volumes
Alaeddin and the Enchanted Lamp; Zein Ul Asnam and The King of the Jinn: (1889) editor and translator
The Persian Letters of Montesquieu (1897) Translator
The Quatrains of Omar Kheyyam of Nisahpour (1898)
Poems of Master François Villon of Paris (1900)
The Poems of Hafiz (1901) A translation in three volumes
Oriental Tales: The Book of the Thousand Nights and One Night (1901) A translation in fifteen volumes
The Descent of the Dove & Other Poems (1902)
Poetical Works (1902) Two volumes
Stories of Boccaccio (1903)
Vigil and Vision: New Sonnets (1903)
Hamid the Luckless & Other Tales in Verse (1904)
Songs of Consolation: New Poems (1904)
Sir Winfrith & Other Poems (1905)
Selections from the Poetry of John Payne (1906) selected by Tracy and Lucy Robinson
Flowers of France: Romantic Period (1906)
Flowers of France, The Renaissance Period (1907)
The Quatrains of Ibn et Tefrid (1908, second edition 1921)
Flowers of France: The Latter Days (1913)
Flowers of France: The Classic Period (1914)
The Way of the Winepress (1920)
Nature and Her Lover (1922)
The Autobiography of John Payne of Villon Society Fame, Poet and Scholar (1926)